IMAGES OF ENGLAND

AROUND
STANNINGTON

IMAGES OF ENGLAND

AROUND
STANNINGTON

STANNINGTON LOCAL HISTORY GROUP

The
History
Press

Frontispiece: The sign on entering Stannington from Bingley Lane stating it is still part of the Wortley District.

First published in 2004 by Tempus Publishing

Reprinted in 2010 by
The History Press
The Mill, Brimscombe Port,
Stroud, Gloucestershire, GL5 2QG
www.thehistorypress.co.uk

British Library Cataloguing in Publication Data.
A catalogue record for this book is available from the British Library.

ISBN 978 0 7524 3372 1

Typesetting and origination by
Tempus Publishing Limited.
Printed and bound in Great Britain by
Marston Book Services Limited, Oxford

Contents

Acknowledgements

We should like to thank all those who have helped us in any way in compiling this book. Our thanks go to those local people of Stannington who have loaned us their precious family photographs and also supplied us with information and comments. This, backed with the benefit of their local knowledge, has proved invaluable.

Our special thanks therefore go to Mr and Mrs A. Abel, Iris Ayres, Rowland and Mavis Brown, Betty Chubb, Brenda Daniels, Kay Drabble, Pauline Glossop, Eileen and Ernest Goodison, Jack Goodison, Eileen Gray, Joan Gray, Marlene and Keith Harper, Pauline Hatcher, Dorothy Helliwell, Rowland and Betty Helliwell, Rene Jackson, John Nichols, Pat Oates, Clarice Robinson, Les Stenton, Freda Vickers and all members of the Stannington Local History Group and the Stannington Players. Our sincere thanks also go to Malcolm Nunn from Bradfield Parish Council, Hillsborough Community Development Trust and Seaman's Photographers. *Walking the Rivelin*, researched by K. Kendall, was used for information on the Rivelin Valley. If we have inadvertently missed anyone, please accept our apologies. We have made every effort to discover the copyright of photographs, but some have been impossible to trace and we give our apologies for any infringements.

Introduction

Stannington still has much the feel of being a village despite the fact it is now joined administratively and physically to the City of Sheffield.

The history of becoming part of Sheffield should be mentioned as it shows the independent nature of Stannington people. In the mid-1960s local people rallied under the Stannington Association to appoint counsel and to rebut the argument put forward by the Sheffield Corporation to include Stannington within the city boundary and build extensively in the Rivelin and Loxley Valleys. At the time Stannington was part of Wortley District Council in the West Riding of Yorkshire. At an unofficial meeting, in a Lomas Hall filled to overflowing, the government inspector, Sir Edward Ritson, sounded out the village feeling about the boundary change. There was no doubt where the strength of feeling lay, but Stannington eventually was included in the Sheffield Metropolitan District, though it remains as a ward in the rural parish of Bradfield. However, the Rivelin Valley and the green belt were saved as no building was allowed. Those of us living in Stannington today have to be thankful for the countryside around us because of that earlier action by its residents of the time. Sheffield itself is often mentioned as being 'a large village', so Stannington could probably be referred to as 'a village within a village', which maybe gives it its sense of individuality.

Stannington as a community has always been strong, as it still is today. As a hill village, in the past it was quite remote and could often be cut off by snow and bad weather in the winters, so people had to rely on one another. In the first half of the twentieth century, and even earlier, the churches, chapels and public houses all provided the villagers with plenty of social and sporting activities. Many cricket and football teams were set up, all playing in different leagues, along with bowling and other sports. Outings were arranged to the country or coast, travelling first by horse bus and later by charabanc. There were the traditions of Cakin in November and the singing of local carols at Christmas in the public houses and in peoples' homes.

All these activities gave people a richer social life and in the 1950s when the Lomas Hall was built, this, the village hall, added so much to Stannington. Being next to the parish church and close to many of the public houses, it became the heart of the village and the venue for so many events. Even though this wasn't a wealthy area, there was plenty for people to be involved in.

This, however, is a long way from the original 'village' which was three separate clusters of dwellings linked by scattered farmhouses. Here the people eked out a precarious living working on small farms and following various trades in the cutlery industry sited in the Rivelin and Loxley valleys, or in out-work in workshops attached to their homes. In subsequent years the wealth of the area gradually increased as the ganister and refractory works grew in importance and the transport links into Sheffield opened up new horizons, but little changed in Stannington itself.

Definite changes began to take place between the wars, when many new houses were built, and after 1945 when the areas between the original settlements were used more and more for new housing, attracting new people to the area and greatly increasing the population. In 2004 only one farm, Fox House Farm on Uppergate Road, remains as a working farm as all the other farms are now part of larger enterprises, or have been pulled down to build housing estates or, as in one case, the local park.

It was thought by the history group that a book of photographs showing the changes would bring back happy memories for older readers and be of interest to newer residents. Unfortunately, quite a few of our archive photographs were not dated or detailed, but the excellent memories of some of our older members (born in Stannington) proved invaluable and they were able to supply much of the missing information. We are also grateful to the people who responded to our request for photographs and we were pleased to include many of them in the book.

I would like to congratulate all the committee for their efforts over the last few months in producing this book, but especially Norma Reaney and Joy Allen-Sissons for their dedicated leadership in bringing this book together.

In conclusion I would like to say how indebted we are to all the people who have helped in the production of this book and we hope you, our readers, will have many hours of pleasure reliving the past or, in the case of younger readers, experiencing an older Stannington.

Doug Broadhead
Chairman
Stannington Local History Group

one

Local
Scenes

A 1973 aerial view of the park showing from left to right the Lomas Hall, the back of the Hare and Hounds and new houses being built on School Lane/Church Street with the cricket pitch in the foreground. Behind Christ Church can be seen the bowling green and to the left of that the children's playground.

Rivelin Glen. On the right is Rivelin Glen Chapel, on the left is Glen Mount. In the 1950s this was a nursery run by Mr and Mrs Smith.

Clod Hall. This name referred to a collection of cottages, not one particular building. They were demolished and are now covered by the Acorn Hill Estate.

Liberty Hill taken from Walkley Bank with Rivelin Valley Road along the bottom, 1920s/1930s. The steep gradient of the hillside is very apparent on this photograph with the path running through the allotments to Roscoe Bank.

Rivelin Paddling Pool, Rivelin Valley Road, *c.* 1958. This was widely used by children during the summer months and is still used today, but not in the same numbers.

RIVELIN. SHEFFIELD 28

The Glen Bridge 'S' bend on Rivelin Valley Road in the early twentieth century showing the Upper Cut Wheel on the left, of which only the fall of water from where the wheel housing had been can now be seen. The cottages in the centre are still there, as is the Rivelin Glen Methodist Chapel, top right.

The Stump Cross, situated at the junction of Stannington Road and Oldfield Road (outside the Sportsman), is by the old Racker Way from Sheffield to Stannington. These rude stone crosses were erected on bridleways and at boundary points in medieval times. The cross marks the boundary of Stannington village. The earliest reference found was in Harrison's survey of 1637, when the cross was described as a 'Stumpe Cross of medieval origin'.

Stannington Road at the top of Fairbarn Road in the 1960s, showing the gable end of the old shop.

The building on the far left was Lockwood's butchers, then Joe Skelton's fruit shop, before becoming Elsie's fruit shop. Next to that was the entrance to the farmyard of the Manor House. The next building shows the window of Levi Revitt's cobblers shop, which had previously belonged to Cobbler Dawson. The cottages on the right are Knowle Top Cottages.

Spout House farm buildings in the 1950s, looking up Spout Lane with Highfield Rise in the distance.

Recently demolished toilets outside Stannington Park on Uppergate Road. The new library was built on this site.

Cricket Ground August 1963

Stannington United Cricket Club ground, 1963.

Cutting through a snow drift 3 March 1908 on Uppergate Road at the top of Bankfield Lane.

Snow cutting on Uppergate Road in the 1920s by the war memorial.

This trough on Tofts Lane, Rivelin, is in the area of a drift road mentioned in the Enclosure Act. It was 'for the use of the inhabitants of Stannington for the convenience of watering their cattle at the watering place'.

two

Buildings

Townhead Farm, Uppergate Road, showing Mr and Mrs Goodison and John Priestley. The farm is thought to have been in the Goodison family for 200 years.

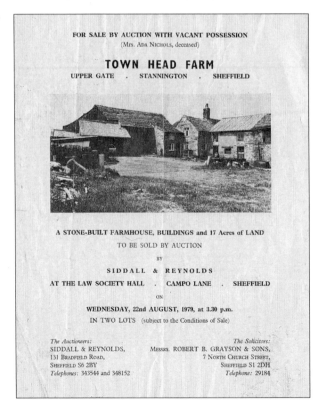

FOR SALE BY AUCTION WITH VACANT POSSESSION
(Mrs. ADA NICHOLS, deceased)

TOWN HEAD FARM

UPPER GATE   .   STANNINGTON   .   SHEFFIELD

A STONE-BUILT FARMHOUSE, BUILDINGS and 17 Acres of LAND

TO BE SOLD BY AUCTION

BY

SIDDALL & REYNOLDS

AT THE LAW SOCIETY HALL   .   CAMPO LANE   .   SHEFFIELD

ON

WEDNESDAY, 22nd AUGUST, 1979, at 3.30 p.m.

IN TWO LOTS (subject to the Conditions of Sale)

The Auctioneers: The Solicitors:
SIDDALL & REYNOLDS,   MESSRS. ROBERT B. GRAYSON & SONS,
131 BRADFIELD ROAD,   7 NORTH CHURCH STREET,
SHEFFIELD S6 2BY   SHEFFIELD S1 2DH
Telephones: 343544 and 348152   Telephone: 29184

Cover of the sale catalogue for Town Head Farm.

Nichols Farm at Knowle Top. The site is near the pavilion in Stannington Park. The old Hare and Hounds is in the background.

Looking down Sheldon Lane with Rushby's shop on the left, and a row of back-to-back cottages on the right-hand side.

Well House Farm, Oldfield Road. The piece of land at the site of the well, which is in front of the fence, in the immediate foreground, is the only piece of common land still in existence in Stannington.

The White House, Nethergate, probably the oldest house in Stannington, could date back to the seventeenth century. It was originally painted white and traces of white paint can still be seen on the mortar.

Above: The war memorial, Lomas Hall and Christ Church taken from Uppergate Road in the 1980s.

Right: A copy of the programme for the official opening of the Lomas Hall on 10 December 1955 by Miss Flora Lomas, who donated the money to build the hall and left a small trust for its maintenance. It is now run by a group of volunteers.

THE LOMAS HALL
STANNINGTON

OFFICIAL
OPENING

on
SATURDAY, DECEMBER 10th, 1955
at 3-0 p.m.

by
MISS LOMAS

The Carlton Press, 172, Langsett Road, Sheffield. &

Houses on the lane behind the Crown and Glove, Uppergate Road, 1975.

Mettam's Yard, Uppergate Road, 1975. The cottages shown were the homes of the Odgen family and Miss Revitt. The building on the right was the wash-house.

Sheldon Lane taken from Stannington Road, with Rushby's shop. This site is now the Rose and Crown car park.

Spout House Farm, *c.* 1960 with Loxley Valley in the distance.

Cottages on Uppergate Road, opposite the medical centre, prior to their restoration. One of these cottages was used as a doctor's surgery.

Two cottages between the Rose and Crown and Rushby's shop on Sheldon Lane, 1973, just before their demolition.

Cottages at Knowle Top, opposite the Peacock Inn, *c.* 1910. The far right cottage was Hayward's shop and the gable end of the post office can be seen behind it. It appears all the inhabitants of these cottages wanted to be in the photograph.

Cottages at Knowle Top, *c.* 1950. Far right is the old post office. The gable end in the centre of the photo is the cottage that was attached to the Peacock Inn. All these properties have now been demolished.

View down the present Greaves Lane (formerly Acorn Hill Lane), at the turn of the century. At that time this area of Stannington was called Han Moor. Note the round fire insurance plaque on the corner of the building, and the water pump on the far right of the photo.

Colin Hayward's butchers shop at the junction of Uppergate Road and Stannington Road, just prior to its demolition in the 1960s.

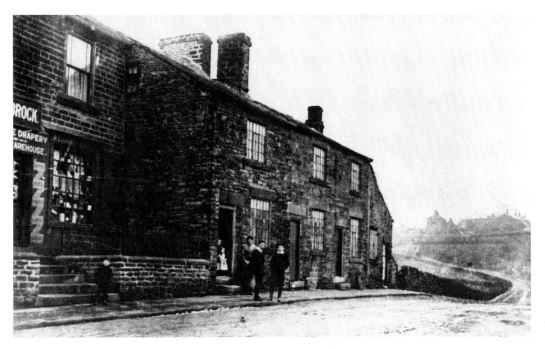

The post office and cottages at Knowle Top looking towards 'Between the Fields'. These buildings were demolished in the 1960s and this is now the site of the library car park.

Cottages at Nook End, at the top of Wood Lane.

Pond Farm showing the cruck construction, prior to its restoration.

Pond Farm on the left, taken from Stannington Park, before it was renovated. The last farmer there was Albert Race with his wife Nancy. On the right is Pond House, occupied for many years by May and Hector Revitt.

Above: The cottages on Stannington Road were called Knowle Top Cottages, but were known by the locals as 'Staring Row'. In the 1980s the far right cottage was demolished, but the remaining four cottages were renovated and converted into two houses. To the left is Arnold Wragg's works.

Right: A prefab at 45 Cliff Road in January 1947. Freda and Arnold Vickers moved there in 1946 just after Arnold was demobbed. In the winter of 1947 they fetched coal on a sledge from the top of Greaves Lane. They moved, *c.* 1960 as the prefabs were supposed to be demolished, but they are still there to this day.

This photograph is taken from Knowle Top Cottages looking up Stannington Road towards Knowle Top.

The demolition of Levi Revitt's cobblers shop on Stannington Road.

Pond Yard Cottages taken from the shops on Stannington Road around 1980 before their renovation.

Croft House, Stannington Road, 1978. This house is approached via a path between the semi-detached houses on the left-hand side of Stannington Road, below the shops, and backs onto Nook End. Owned by the Barket family.

Alpha House in the mid-1940s. This was taken before the corner of the garden was removed to widen Oldfield Road. Above Alpha House is the public footpath that leads to the buildings that were used by the Oates family as a cutlery manufacturing workshop. Later it was used by Stafford Bennet, in the name of Panda Press.

Cottages, known as 'The Fold' just off Stannington Road on the public footpath from Stannington Road to the side of Alpha House on Oldfield Road. Mrs Broomhead lived in the first house and the Moodys lived in the second house.

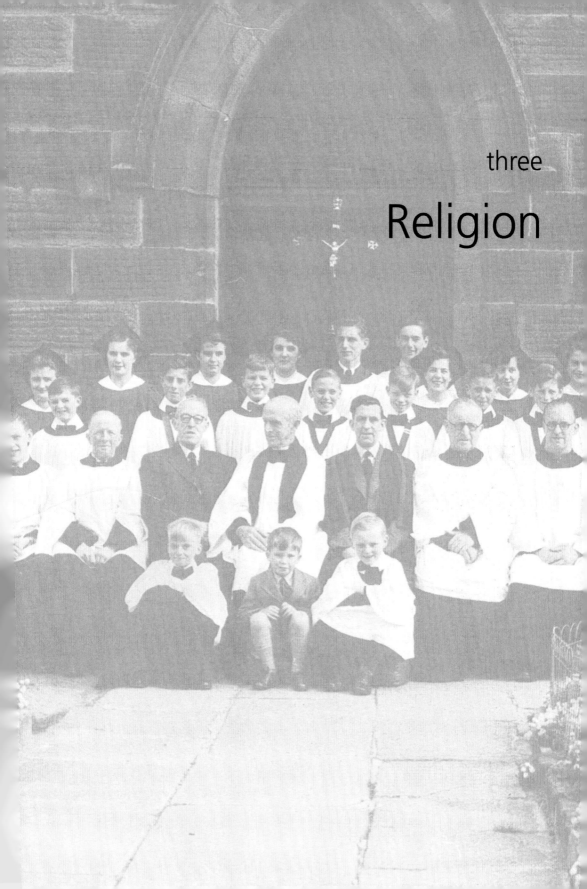

three

Religion

Underbank Chapel: The present chapel was built in 1741 by Mr Thomas Marriott. This replaced the original building on land given by Richard Spoone in 1652. It was the first place of worship in Stannington.

Underbank schoolroom, across the road from the chapel. It was built in 1854, replacing the original built in 1654, which was the only day school in Stannington. It was closed as a day school in July 1911, but continued to be used as a Sunday school.

Underbank Chapel Women's League knitting group in the early 1930s. In the middle of the back row is Ann Goodison (née Wilson).

Underbank ladies at a church tea. Second from the left is Mrs Turner.

Ladies outside Underbank Chapel in the early twentieth century.

Right: Mr Iden Payne, Underbank Unitarian Minister 1884–1905.

Below: Underbank Chapel Sunday school pantomime.

A picture of Underbank Chapel, sewn by Inday Oates in 1848, where it hung for many years until being stolen. Inday Oates' grave lies near to the chapel door.

Clarice Robinson (*née* Harper), Underbank harvest queen 1938, with Joe Gray, cushion-bearer. Clarice was crowned by Miss Flora Lomas. (Printed by kind permission of Seaman Photographers, Sheffield)

Underbank Chapel after the removal of the organ to the right-hand side in 1952. The chapel has been altered extensively inside over the years but has not changed externally.

The organ in Underbank Chapel which was replaced by a new one in 1921 as a war memorial to the men of the First World War. It was moved to the right-hand side of the chapel in 1952.

Stannington Methodist Chapel was opened in 1879 after the original building of 1822 was demolished. The chapel was rededicated in October 2004, after being closed for twenty years.

Men working behind the Methodist Chapel clearing space for extending the graveyard.

A pipe organ was installed in the Methodist Chapel in 1899.

Knowle Top Methodist Anniversary Sermons for 1930.

Stannington Methodist school – scholars and teachers.

Stannington Methodist Chapel, and the crowning of the Sunday school queen Vera Hadfield in 1948. The retiring queen is Mavis Horton.

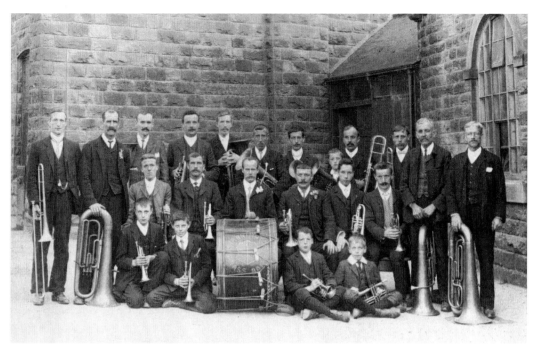

Stannington Band outside Knowle Top Chapel pre-1913.

Stannington Methodist Chapel orchestra and choir at the opening of the new Chapel in 1878.

Knowle Top Methodist Sunday school concert 1923. Second on the left on the second row is Ernest Spencer.

Methodist Sunday school annual outing to Castleton, *c.* 1930.

Christ Church, Stannington before the Lych Gate was in place.

Above: Christ Church, Stannington. The church was built from the 'Million Fund' and was consecrated in July 1830. Curates were appointed to the church until 1843, when Stannington became a parish and was entitled to its own vicar.

Left: Christ Church, Stannington, *c.* 1900: At this time the organ was in the balcony and the choir sang from there.

Christ Church, Stannington, decorated for the Harvest Festival, *c.* 1930. Gas lighting was installed in 1929. Note the side balconies and two pulpits.

This photograph shows the side balconies in situ at Stannington church, *c.* 1900. The font in the middle aisle was replaced by the Angel Font in 1945 (provided by Sunday school scholars, past and present), and removed to the churchyard. It was stolen from there in 2001.

The dedication of the war memorial in 1921.

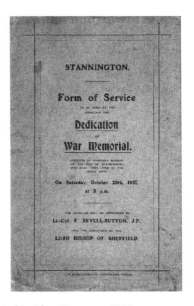

Above left: Stannington War Memorial in the making at Rivelin Glen Quarry, *c.* 1920.

Above right: Form of service for the dedication of the war memorial, Saturday 29 October 1921.

Above: Stannington Brass Band at the Armistice Day service, *c.* 1930. The vicar is the Revd F.A. Stebbing. The two boys on the right behind the vicar are Rowland Helliwell and Harry Thorpe.

Right: This font was brought by Revd Gill from Bradfield Church in 1827 and was used until a new font, given by the combined efforts of those baptised in the church, was dedicated on 21 July 1945. The stone font was then installed as a feature in the churchyard but sadly was stolen in 2001.

The Revd Samuel Robinson Carver was appointed as incumbent by the benefactors who built the vicarage. He and his wife were tragically killed when their horse and carriage ran away and crashed at Malin Bridge.

The May Queen of Stannington Church School, c. 1930. From left to right: Kathleen May, Dorothy Crookes, Mary Elliott, Gladys Wright, Stuart Furness, Walter Wragg, Mary Furness (new queen), Madge White (retiring queen), Clem Furness, -?-, -?-, Maggie Davidson, -?-, Jean Allison. The eight girl attendants wore pale green dresses decorated with butterflies.

The gravestone of Mina Dyson, who wrote the carol Stannington, the first few bars of which are on the stone: 'Sing all ye people of the earth today'. Stannington carols are sung today in churches, pubs and many other gatherings.

Christ Church Stannington choir, 1955. From left to right, back row: Christine Wragg, Jean Garton, Pam Sherratt, Margaret Hodgett, Margaret Flewitt, Ann Doubleday, Josie Coulson, John Burton, David Wragg, Kathleen Grayson, Muriel Furness, Ruth Standing, Dorothy Nichols, Ann Mosley, Janet Mosley. Middle row: Brian Pendall, John Hall, -?-, Roddy Taylor, Jimmy White, Nick Farrelly, John Clayton, Leslie Coulson, Steven Staniforth, Peter Mosley, Michael Comley, Michael Johnson, Roger Wheywell, David Wilson. Sitting: Mr Betts, Cyril Stanley, Brian Medley, Mr Stafford, Mr Rhodes, Revd Stebbing, Edward Hall, Wilton Wilde, Nelson Hall, Mr Skelton, Harold Mosley. Boys: Richard Comley, Geoffrey Hall, Ian Mosley.

In 1913 the King Edward VII Hospital was built in Rivelin (originally known as the Sheffield Cripples' Home). In 1924 there was the first Whit Sunday procession to the hospital, followed in 1926 by the gift of eggs. Here is Stannington Brass Band outside the church hall preparing to lead the walk down to Rivelin.

Singing round the wards with the band, conducted by Mr H.E. Hall.

Stannington Girls Brigade members, c. 1935. From left to right: Kathleen May, Mary Goodison, Connie Burgin, Jean Allison.

A shire horse memorial gravestone in Stannington churchyard in memory of Thomas Gosney, who died 9 October 1944, aged seventy-three years. He bred and broke in horses, some for Daniel Doncaster, the steel makers, until the company became mechanised.

Mrs Priestley (right), a teacher at the Stanningron Church School, with her sister Miss Kate Wragg, who became a missionary in Zululand pre-1914.

Stannington Church choir with the Revd Gamaliel Milner, *c.* 1910. Mr Reuben Gray (schoolmaster) is on the left-hand side of the top row.

Bowcroft Cemetery, known locally as the 'Quakers' Burial Ground', is now a small plantation in a high and windswept spot. Surrounded by a stone wall, five gravestones of the Shaw family from the eighteenth century lie together.

The Catholic school on Nethergate, now a private house, is on the site of the old Nethergate Hall, the home of the Revell family, who removed to Revell Grange in 1742 after the death of Rowland Revell. Mass was celebrated here in this rather wild and lonely place as there was less chance of discovery. The chapel later became St Mary's Roman Catholic School.

Revell Grange, the home of the Revell family from the early fifteenth century, with an integral chapel used for the celebration of Holy Mass in secret. Note the cross above the site of the chapel in the house.

four

Education

Left: Underbank School: A new school was opened in 1854 to replace the first school of 1652. George Revitt was the master and received £20 per annum. He had to have the building whitewashed once a year at his own expense.

Below: Underbank Chapel and schoolroom looking across to Storrs. The day school was established in 1652, and later rebuilt. The current building was opened in May 1854 accompanied by a public tea party – tickets were 1s 6d.

Pupils and teachers at Underbank School, *c.* 1900. Mr Haigh is on the right.

A group of children with Mrs Payne, appointed in 1899 to Underbank School. The school was closed in 1911 and Mrs Payne and the children moved to the new council school in the centre of the village. She became headmistress of the infant department until her retirement in 1924.

Left: Miss Sarah Sykes, head teacher at the Methodist School 1875–1905.

Below: Methodist School concert May Day celebration.

Cantata, *The Ambulance Maids*, Stannington Methodist School, *c.* 1905. Seventh from the left is Clara Francis, who was born in 1894.

Cantata, around 1918–20. A group of boys from the Methodist School, performing *Gun Drill*.

A view of Stannington Church School, School Lane, leading to Oldfield Road and Nethergate. All the surrounding fields have been extensively built on. The solitary house on the corner was occupied by Alex Oxley and his wife. He virtually reconstructed the church clock and looked after it until his death in 1974.

Stannington Church School, Class Four, c. 1900. The headmaster is Mr Reuben Gray and fourth from the left on the front row is Lillian Nichols.

Violin class at the Council School. Third from right on the back row is Thomas Francis, who was born in 1895.

A class in Stannington Church School. The headmaster, Mr Reuben Gray, is on the left of the picture and Miss Kate Wragg, teacher, is on the right. Miss Wragg went as a missionary to Zululand pre-1914 and remained there until her death.

An aerial view of Stannington Junior and Infant School, *c.* 1956.

Looking down Uppergate Road. The present primary school, known first as the Council School, was built in 1911 on the field in the left of the picture. The library, police houses and medical centre were built on the fields opposite at a later date. The near-view cottages, extensively modernised, are still in situ.

Pupils at Stannington Council School in 1919. On the second row fourth from the left is Myrtle Goodison.

five

People

Above: The Wood family at Stannington Wood Farm, *c.* 1910: From left to right, back row: Willis Wood, Lucy Wood. Front row: Ada Wood, Wilfred Wood, Doris Wood, Mrs Wood, Lily Wood. The farm on Stanwood Road fell into disrepair but the farmhouse and outbuildings have now been renovated and converted into flats and houses.

Left: Mr and Mrs Barker, Knowle Top Cottages, which were opposite Knowle Top Chapel, Uppergate Road, where the library is now, early 1900s. Note the next-door neighbour peeping round the doorway.

Right: The cover of the rule book of the Domestic Funeral Society which commenced on 14 April 1845. It is not known how long the society was in existence.

Below: The Ladies' Funeral Club from the Hare and Hounds on their annual trip to the seaside in the 1930s: From left to right, back row: Mrs Winkley, Mrs Gilman, Mrs Gray, Mrs Lawson, Mrs Hague, -?-, -?-, -?-, -?-, -?-, -?-, Mrs Mettam, Mrs Skelton, -?-, Mrs Dyson, Mrs Mallinson, -?-. Front row: Coach driver (possibly Warriner's Coaches), Miss Furness, Mrs Goodison, -?-, Mrs Vickers, Mrs Taylor, Mrs Revitt, Mrs Grayson and child, -?-. Children crouching at the front: Donald Gray, Ernest Gillespie, Ronald Grayson, Clifford Mettam, -?-, Florence Winkley, Vera Revitt.

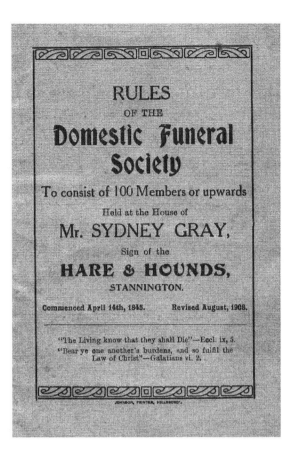

RULES
OF THE
Domestic Funeral Society

To consist of 100 Members or upwards

Held at the House of

Mr. SYDNEY GRAY,

Sign of the

HARE & HOUNDS,
STANNINGTON.

Commenced April 14th, 1845.   Revised August, 1908.

"The Living know that they shall Die"—Eccl. ix, 5.
"Bear ye one another's burdens, and so fulfil the Law of Christ"—Galatians vi. 2.

JOHNSON, PRINTER, HILLSBORO'.

Left: Christ Church, Stannington. Bride Connie Burgin with stepfather William Allison, 30 March 1946.

Below: Wedding at Underbank Unitarian Chapel, 8 October 1937. From left to right: Walter Goodison, Ann Goodison, Iden Goodison (groom), Dorothy May Tomkin (bride), Mrs Tomkin, Len Wilson, -?-, Jack Tomkin.

Above: The wedding of Rosemary Dyson and Jack Goodison took place at Christ Church on 5 July 1941. After Mary's death in 1991 Jack compiled his collection of local carols, arranged annual music concerts in the Lomas Hall and held plant sales all in aid of Weston Park Hospital and St Luke's Hospice in her memory. To date he has raised £25,000 and a plaque has been placed in the Lomas Hall to commemorate this achievement.

Right: Frank Oglesby Hall, verger and sexton at Christ Church Stannington for thirty-one years. He died 24 February 1939 aged sixty-nine.

Above: Stannington Tennis Club, *c.* 1940. From left to right, back row: Eric Stebbings, Hector Gray, Fred Winfield, Arthur Comley, Ernest Goodison, Charles Kenneth, 'Bobbins' Fields, Geoff Ridal, Doug Hides, Dorothy Garton. Front row: Kathleen May, Joan Birch, Connie Elderkin, Olive Grayson, Jean Allison, Irene Mettam, Flora Gray.

Left: Sydney, John and Lily, the children of Sydney and Mary Ann Gray. The Gray family were at the Hare and Hounds for sixty-seven years from 1895-1962. Sydney died after being landlord for only three years and his widow kept the pub until 1921 with the help of her sons. John Gray died after three years as licensee then Syd Gray took over from 1924-1962.

The Woodland View section of the ARP, taken at the end of the Second World War. The gentleman smoking a pipe is William Youle and his wife, Edith Youle (*née* Dyson), is fourth from the right on the row below. A friend of theirs, second from the right on the same row is Mrs Gell. Note the boy on the left with the tin helmet on!

Stannington Home Guard, taken outside Underbank Chapel school room in the 1940s. From left to right, back row (heads): Bob Wragg, John Jowle, Jennings (Kirk), Brian Russell, -?-, Nelson Froggatt, -?-, -?-, Walter Wragg, George Nichols, -?-. Third row (shoulders): -?-, Harry Gray, -?-, -?-, Colin Spencer, Bill Dawson, ? Glossop, Bill Wallis, Tom Stephens, Sam Dawson. Second row (sitting): -?-, W. Ibbotson, Ernest Harper, Bill Goodison, -?-, Sir Richard Hughes, -?-, Eric Goodlad, Don Harper, Royce North. Front row (crossed legs): Jeff Barker, Desmond Horsfield, Cyril Riley, (Old) George Guite, John Crookes.

Above and below: Stannington clinic held at Underbank, *c.* 1939. The photos show healthy looking children with smart, well-dressed mums, at a time before the National Health Service came into being in 1948.

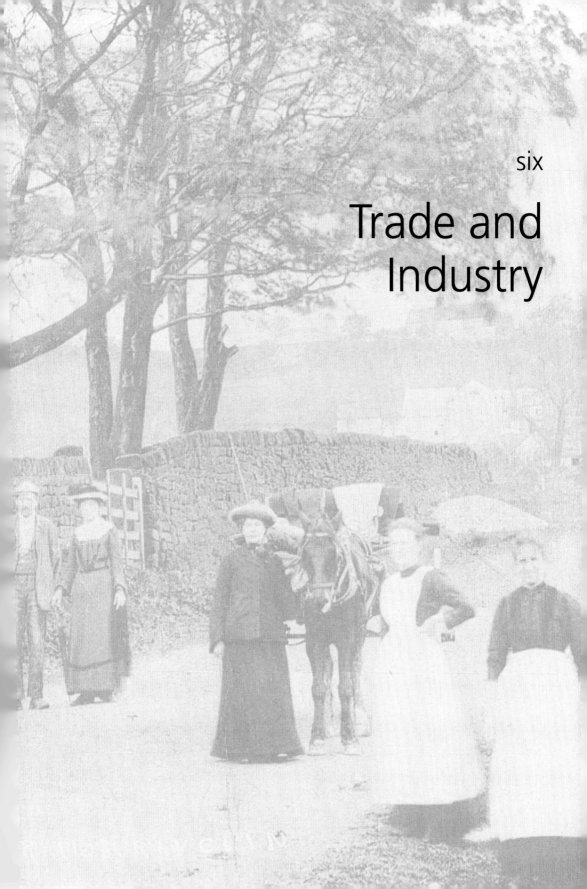

six

Trade and
Industry

Spooner's Wheels, Rivelin Valley, owned by the Spooner family in 1794. The grinding of files, saws, scythes and cutlery was carried out and part of the mill was used to forge knives. The Spooner's Wheels were worked until 1930. These mills were sited where the café is now – between the children's paddling pool and the playground.

The Hollins Mill (or Rivelin Bridge Mill), in the 1900s. In 1868 the mill was converted to a corn mill owned by John Wilson. It was closed in 1909. The mill buildings have now gone, but the weir on the Rivelin is still impressive. The Holly Bush Inn stands in the background.

The two-storey cutler's shop built in the early nineteenth century in the small croft below Pond Farm was occupied by brothers George and Sam Vickers. They used one storey each, and like other cutlers took their week's work to Sheffield at the weekend. Later generations of the Vickers family used the workshop as a razor scale presser's shop.

'Ronksleys' end cottage and the blacksmith's shop were demolished for road widening in the 1960s. In the row only the Peacock Inn survives. Knowle Top Methodist Chapel is on the left.

The Cotterills of Little Matlock, in the 1920s. From left to right: Willis Cotterill, Levi Cotterill, Walter Cotterill and George Cotterill, with what appears to be a new steam lorry. It would be used in the loading of ganister which had been quarried for use in the steel industry. The dog just raises its head to be included in the photograph.

Loading ganister at the cliff top below the Robin Hood Inn, near Myers Grove Lane in the early twentieth century. The ganister would be used as a flux in the steel-making industry.

Rivelin Glen Quarry.

Henry Gosney and Sons, Rivelin Glen Lorries, worked from Rivelin Glen Quarry. William Allison dressed all the stone used to build Rivelin post office. From left to right: Arthur Gosney, John Edward Gosney, -?- , -?-, Bill Allison, Harry Allison, Tommy Booth, William Allison.

Len and Bernard Earnshaw of Stannington delivering coal by steam engine in the early 1900s.

The wheelwright's shop, taken 1963, was opposite Knowle Top Methodist chapel. It was later used by Norman Charlesworth as a joiner's shop.

Workmen at Drabble's Brickworks, Brookside, c. 1915. Bricks are stacked high in front of the kiln. The bricks on the left-hand barrow were called 'runners'. These were used for pouring molten steel into the moulds.

Thomas Wragg's works, Loxley Valley in the 1930s. It is thought that Thomas Wragg discovered the famous Stannington pot clay around 1830 on his land at Beacon Wood. There were other beds of clay in the Sheffield area, but Stannington was considered to be the best. This started the refractory businesses in the area. The brick-making sheds can be seen here and to the left is a round kiln under the chimney. The offices were in the houses on the far right and the workers' cottages back right.

Workers of J. & J. Dyson refractories in the early 1930s, taken in front of a kiln.

Dyson's refractories, Stannington, famous for making bricks for lining the furnaces in steel-making. In the mid-nineteenth century Stannington pot clay was found to be an ideal refractory both for the old Crucible steel-making process and the new Bessemer process which was spreading rapidly in the Sheffield area. This gave employment to many local people and Dyson's, situated just outside the village at Stopes, became a very successful company. They are still trading to this day.

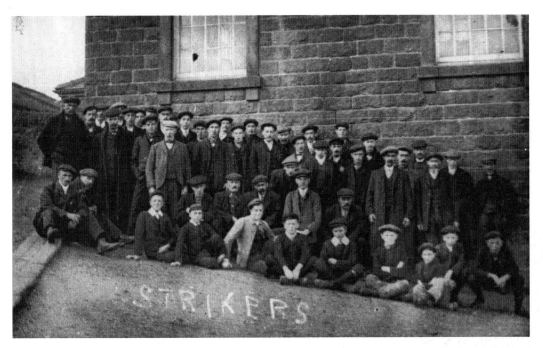

Brickyard strikers, 1912. Taken outside Underbank Chapel schoolroom, most likely they were workers from J. & J. Dyson.

Thomas Wragg employees, c. 1930.

Rushby's shop on Sheldon Lane.

Mr and Mrs William Rhodes' shop on Nethergate, which is now a private house. The shop sold groceries and was a general store. It remained in the Rhodes family until the 1960s.

Right: Mallinson's Butchers, *c.* 1920, adjoining the Peacock Inn yard. Seen here are Wycliffe Mallinson and Ernest Revitt. Eventually the shop became Elsie's fruit shop.

Below: The post office on Uppergate Road at Knowle Top.

Left: The Little Park area of Stannington showing the Co-op, chip shop and Harrison's general store in 1950-51, before the cobbler's/wool shop, fruit and handyman buildings were built.

Below: Fearn's shop on Stannington Road (just below the infant school), was a general store until the 1980s. Next to it was Phyllis Hague's hairdressers shop. Both shops are now private houses.

Right: The rulebook of the Friendly and Charitable Society of Trademen in Stannington, printed in 1875.

Below: Hand bellows and the hearth to the right in the smithy adjacent to the Peacock Inn.

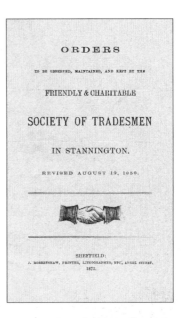

ORDERS

TO BE OBSERVED, MAINTAINED, AND KEPT BY THE

FRIENDLY & CHARITABLE

SOCIETY OF TRADESMEN

IN STANNINGTON.

REVISED AUGUST 12, 1858.

SHEFFIELD:
J. ROBERTSHAW, PRINTER, LITHOGRAPHER, ETC., ANGEL STREET,
1875.

The new motor-bus service for Rivelin, 1913. Rivelin post office is on the right and Rails Road, which leads to Stannington, can be seen at the top left.

This photo of Rails Road, Rivelin, was taken in 1907 before the New Road was made. Ponies and traps seem to be the transport of the day, or 'shanks' pony' if you weren't so lucky!

Vincent Drabble and Mr Marsh in a pony and trap at Brookside Farm.

Rivelin Valley Road, 1913. The first bus along the newly constructed road. This photograph also shows a few of the 700 lime trees purchased to line the road and the surrounding areas at a cost of £147. Rivelin Valley Road was built by the Statutory Water Company.

Above: The Oates family, taken at 47 Rivelin Park Road. From left to right, back row: Harry (1891-1970), Rosa (1862-1947), married to Frederick (1860-1923). Front row: Frank (1885-1965), Albert (1898-1936), George (1889-1953).

Left: Albert's son Frederick William Oates, born 20 January 1860, died 17 November 1923 was also a cutler. He returned to live in the Stannington area around 1890 to Rivelin Park Road, which became the home of his descendants until 1996.

Sheffield penknives mainly made by Albert Oates, whose works were established in St Philips Road in 1855. Early members of the Oates family had lived and worked in Stannington as cutlers from the seventeenth to the nineteenth centuries.

The front elevation of 47 Rivelin Park Road, the Oates family home.

Mr Bert Priestly of Otter and Priestly Motor Company, Hanmoor, *c.* 1960.

Bill Otter, in 1953, with a coach on his way back from one of the many fishing trips.

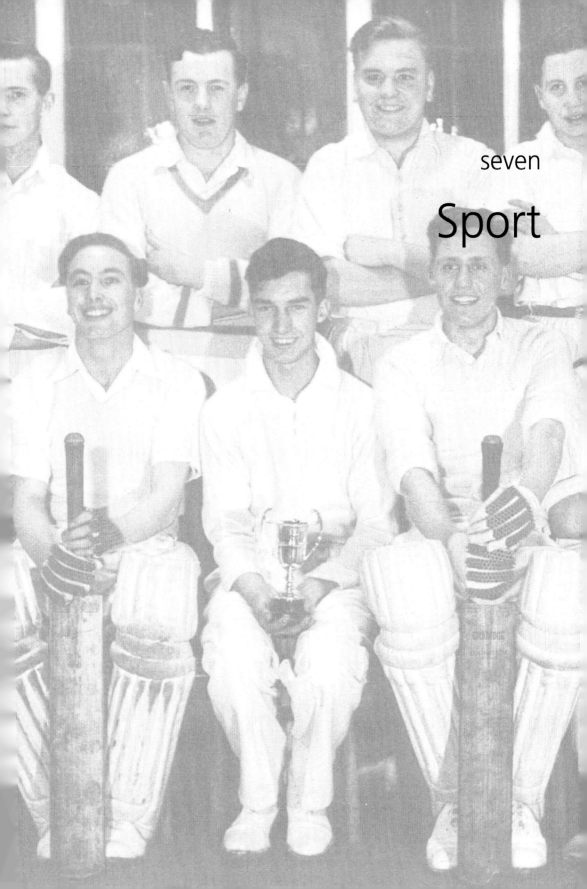

Stannington Bowling Club in the 1950s. From left to right, back row: Joe Gray, Derek Turner, Doug Emsall, Bill Wallis, ? Nichols, Ken Grayson, Stuart Wilmot, John Gray. Front row: Harold Grayson, Granville Vickers, Wycliffe Harper, Horace Goodison, Sidney Hague, Harold Nichols, Harold Harper, Derek Nichols, Kenneth Smith, Stan Harper, -?-, Harry Becker, Laurie Goodison.

Stannington Bowling Club was formed in 1906. The green they played on until 1972 was behind the Peacock Inn. A green was provided for them in Stannington Park when Wortley council needed the land previously used to build sheltered accommodation. This photo was taken c. 1920. From left to right, back row: J. Dyson, -?-, W. Abel, William Mettam, E. Bramall. Third row: Mr Peaston (Underbank minister), Alf ?, Willis Womack (landlord of the Peacock), Sid Marsh, George Vickers, Charlie Furness, Bill Coggins. Second row: John Gilman, Thomas Fearn, -?-, George Revitt, William Lomas, Chas Lomas, Henry Wright, Wilf Lawson. Front row, Tom Furness, Edward Gilman, Colin Goodison, Frank Ibbotson, ? Bradshaw, J. Harrison, J. Worthington, E. Revitt, Harold Womack.

Little Matlock Cricket Match, 1950s. The Little Matlock Cricket Club was formed in 1925. Loxley village can be seen in the distance across the valley.

The Robin Hood Cricket Team, 9 July 1954.

Stannington United Cricket Club, winners of the Rotherham and District League, 1909 season. From left to right, back row: J. Barker, H. Beachell, B. Lawson, J. Hawksworth, A. Harper, F.W. Harper, F. Dronfield, H. Helliwell, A. Nichols, A. Harper. Front row: F. Marsden, E. Dyson, S. Inman, H. Wilmot, G. Marsden, W. Tattershall, W.C. Goodison, J. Rose, J. Brocklehurst.

Stannington United Cricket Club annual dinner and trophy presentation 1953 in the Hare and Hounds. Among those present is Syd Gray (landlord), holding cups are John Gray, Ken Smith and W. Wallis. Others present are Glad Turner, Micky Grayson, A. Becker, Colin Gillott, B. Jones, S. Harper, Raymond Turner, D. Turner, Joe Gray, Harry Wright, Edmund Wright, E. Hogg, L. Jones, Harold Harper, S. Nichols, W. Booth and L. Webster.

Stannington United Cricket Club, 1975, Sheffield League Division 'A'. From left to right, back row: Gordon Bartholomew, K. Raw, P. Baxter, Fred Marsden (umpire), C. Ellison, D. Dobing, J.G. Gray. Front row: D. Simpson, T. Whittaker, T. Haddington, S. Harper, K. Grayson (captain), D. Turner.

From left to right, back row: Councillor H.E. Wright, E. Pashley (chairman), E. Hogg (secretary), S. Gray, A. Pashley. Front row: S. Harper (winner of Fielding Cup), W. Wallis (winner of the Batting Cup), J. Gray (second eleven captain, with the Oates-Harrison Cup) and K. Smith (winner of the Bowling Cup), December 1953.

Above: Stannington Cricket Club in 1940s. From left to right, back row: Gordon Biggins, Peter Stebbing, Alf Fearnley, Joe Gray, Eric Elliott, Ken Grayson. Front row: Denis Nichols, Terry Smith, Derek Turner, Ken Smith, Arthur Becker, Ron Fearnley, Keith Timms.

Left: An informal shot of members in the 1940s. From left to right, back row: -?-, Arthur Becker, Joe Gray, -?-, Colin Gillot. Front row: Derek Nichols, Wally Booth, Donald Gray. Stannington United Cricket Club is the oldest recorded club in the village. The actual date of its formation is difficult to ascertain as all records prior to 1907 were destroyed. However, Hallam quotes a game played against Stannington in 1805 which would date the club to the beginning of the nineteenth century, or may be even earlier.

Above: Members of the Sheffield United Harriers. Number 116 is Willis Horton of Stannington, the winner of the 1923 Hallam Chase. He won many more events and was an all-round sportsman, playing cricket for Dyson's brickyard team, where he worked. He was a football referee and a member of the Stannington Bowling Club. Born in 1902, he died in 1996, aged ninety-three.

Right: John Nichols of Stannington was a member of Sheffield United Harriers, who were winners of National Championships in 1948, 1949, 1956, 1959. He has represented Yorkshire and Northern Counties at cross country on many occasions. In 1956 he was awarded his England 'B' team international shirt. He won the Youth and Junior Championships twice. He is seen here in 1955 when he was the Northern Counties Six-mile Champion. He was Yorkshire Six-mile Champion twice, and the Ten-mile Champion twice.

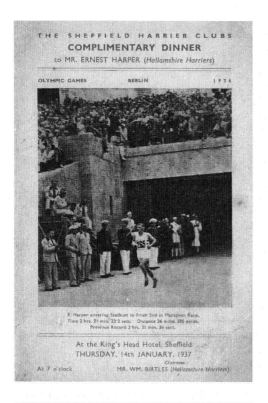

THE SHEFFIELD HARRIER CLUBS
COMPLIMENTARY DINNER
to MR. ERNEST HARPER (Hallamshire Harriers)

OLYMPIC GAMES   BERLIN   1936

E. Harper entering Stadium to finish 2nd in Marathon Race.
Time 2 hrs. 31 mins. 23·2 secs. Distance 26 miles 385 yards.
Previous Record 2 hrs. 31 min. 36 secs.

At the King's Head Hotel, Sheffield
THURSDAY, 14th JANUARY, 1937

At 7 o'clock   *Chairman* : MR. WM. BIRTLES (Hallamshire Harriers)

E. HARPER.
INTERNATIONAL CROSS COUNTRY CHAMPION 1926.
TEN MILES A.A.A. CHAMPION 1926.

Above: Ernest Harper as he won his silver medal at the 1936 Olympic Games in Berlin. He ran second to Son of Japan. At a complimentary dinner in his honour he was presented with the deeds of a house in Stannington, which had been purchased by public subscription. In 1959 he and his wife followed their children to live in Australia, where he died aged seventy-seven.

Left: Ernest Harper, Stannington's most famous son, was a member of the Hallamshire Harriers and represented Britain in the Paris (1924), Amsterdam (1928) and Berlin (1936) Olympic Games. In total he represented England eleven times in international sports events. He was born at Clay Cross, near Chesterfield in 1902 and came to live in Stannington when young. He was a former employee of Thomas Wragg's.

Stannington United Football Club First Eleven, Sheffield and Hallam Amateur League, in the mid–1930s. The colours were green with red collar and sleeves. From left to right, back row: B. Heap, N. Endersby (trainer), Syd Gray (president), W.L. Wingfield, H. Harper, C. Bancroft, O.H. Packham, W. Furness, Albert Stocks (chairman), W. Greaves. Front row: -?-, B. Bishop, F. Heap (who had trials with Sheffield Wednesday), W. Harper, C. Burgin, -?-, Eric Stocks. This picture was taken on the top side of the cricket field. The Crown and Glove is top right.

Stannington church football team for 1925, taken outside the Church school. The Revd F.A. Stebbings is far right in the straw boater. He was the chairman/president of the club. Others present: Frank Hall (secretary) with cap, Frank Hall Jnr, Bob Jones, H. Mosley, Dick Jones, Sid Hague, Hugh Hague, Gilbert Hall.

Stannington Underbank Sunday School Football Club in the 1920s.

J. & J. Dyson football team in the 1950s. From left to right, back row: Alf Gillott, Luther Wright, Jack Stringer, Harold Turner, Colin Spencer, Willis Bell. Front row, Marriot Horsefield, Nelson Hall, Win Wood, Billy Revitt, -?-.

Stannington United Football Club. The headquarters and dressing room were at the Hare and Hounds public house. This photo is the first eleven team from the mid-1920s. The shirts were made of heavy wool. From left to right, back row: J. Marsden, J. Harrison, H. Gilman, J. Baldwin, J. Middlemiss, W. Lawson, -?-, -?-, -?-, -?-, -?-, W. Revitt, ? Milner. Front row: J.F. Hirst (trainer), -?-, -?-, -?-, -?-, -?-, -?-.

Stannington Boys' Club football team 1937/38, taken at Endcliffe Park (where they were beaten 14–1). From left to right, back row: Cyril Riley, Geoff Kirkby, Hector Gray, Geoff Rydal, Doug Stebbings, Roy Wagstaff, Tommy Gosney, Bill Wallis (trainer). Front row: Leonard Furness, Jim Furness, William Gosney, Len Johnson, Joe Atkins.

The kennels at the top of Reynard Lane/Uppergate where the main pack for the Stannington Hunt were kept. The records of the hunt, which was a foot pack, go back to 1892, but it was disbanded after the First World War.

The grave of John Ollerenshaw in Stannington churchyard. He was huntsman of the Stannington Harriers for over fifty years and his tomb was erected by Friends of the Stannington Hunt as a mark of his faithful service. He was born in 1800 and died 5 March 1881.

WINES & SPIRITS

BILLIARDS

JOHN, HENRY, WATERHOUSE.
SPIRITS ALE BEER PORT

eight

Public Houses

The Robin Hood Inn, Little Matlock. The cottages on the left were pulled down in the 1960s and 1970s. This pub was built in 1804 by the Revd Thomas Halliday, originally as a private house. Sheffield Rifle Club used the Robin Hood as its headquarters for many years until the rifle range, in the wood nearby, was closed down.

Robin Hood Fishing Club. The man with a jug by his left knee was George Glossop, who at one time was a steel warehouse foreman/crane driver at the English Steel Corporation, Holme Lane. The pub was run by the Furness family for a long time and the sign above the doorway shows Elizabeth Furness was licensee. Presumably this was after her husband Matthew had died. The picture above this sign has the inscription: 'You gentlemen and archers good, come in and drink with Robin Hood, if Robin Hood be not home, come in and drink with Little John.'

The original Sportsman's Inn at the junction of Stannington Road and Oldfield Road was the first building on the village side of the Stannington and Sheffield boundary.

The demolition of the old Sportman's Inn at the junction of Oldfield Road and Stannington Road, 1966.

Left: Outside the Sportsman's Inn, *c.* 1920. Willis Gray the landlord is on the left with L. Hickinson on the right. Mr Hickinson was a builder and he lived next door to the Sportman's.

Below: The old Hare and Hounds on Uppergate Road. The first mention of this public house appears in the will of Mr Edward Nichols, dated 21 October 1790, when he bequeathed the residue of a 999-year lease on the premises. At that time the house was known as 'Well Green House' but was later known under the sign of the 'Blue Boar'. The name Hare and Hounds goes back at least as far as 1837. The public house was purchased by John Smiths Brewery in 1900. The Gray family kept this public house for a number of years, hence this part of Uppergate Road being known locally as 'Gray's Hill'.

From left to right: Sydney Gray, Rush Wood and Ted Burgin, goalkeeper for Sheffield United in the 1950s and also England B team goalkeeper. Sydney Gray was the landlord of the old Hare and Hounds from 1924 until his death in 1962.

Hare and Hounds customers in the 1940s. Syd Gray the landlord is standing in the middle centre (wearing waistcoat).

Stannington Bowling Club Dinner at the Peacock Inn in 1921.

The British Legion, *c.* 1920 outside the Peacock Inn.

According to the deeds, the Crown and Glove was at one time a cottage in a row of four, serving ale. It was then known as the Tontine – a name given to houses where the owners had each subscribed to the capital required for the purchase, the last survivor inheriting. From 1842 this public house was known as the Crown and Glove, and it passed from the ownership of Bradley and Co. to S.H. Ward and Co. Ltd in 1876. The property was improved in 1962. This is the only public house in the country of this name, but is known locally as the 'Top House'.

A coach trip leaving from the Rose and Crown (Minnie's) car park, c. 1940. Knowle Top Methodist Chapel can be seen in the background. John Bramhall and Reggie Stocks are among those on the outing.

'Regulars' outside Rivelin Hotel, c. 1950. From left to right, back row: Jack Birch, –?–, William Allison, Harvey Gillott, William Burgin. Front row: –?–, –?–.

Outside Rivelin Hotel, c. 1945. William Allison is sitting on the pavement edge far right. The man behind him wearing the cap is William Burgin.

nine

Traditions and Events

Stannington Youth Club Ramblers
– a few of its members in the Lake
District, 1950. From left to right:
Brian Stead, Jim Smith, Alf Lomax,
Wilson Smith, Derek Bygate, Alan
Englert, Roy Mayos, Bob Marshall.

Stannington Local History Group
outing to Thorseby Hall, August
1968.

Stannington Youth Club Ramblers
– more of its members in the Lake
District, 1950. From left to right:
Sheila Warriner, Audrey Wallis, Jean
Mayos, Jean Memmot, Esme Stead,
-?-, Alf Lomax.

Stannington Rag Day, October 1951. The youth club float, 'Samson and Delilah'. From left to right: John Clayton, Maureen Cuttings, Betty Wragg, Keith Timms, Rita Barge, Brian Betts, Harold Horsfield, Pauline Cooper.

Stannington Youth Club First Birthday Party, 1951. From left to right, top row: Mr Barker, Rita Barge, Pat Goodlad, Audrey Wallis, Betty Wragg, John Nichols, Alan Day, Derek Bygate, Jean Collet, Esme Stead, Shirley Wilkinson, Audrey Collet, Tony Skelton. Second row: Margaret Horsfield, Yvonne Malone, Bob Marshall, Wilson Smith, Alan Englert, Ken Strawson, John Tomlinson, Brian Ollerenshaw, Peter Loftus, Harold Horsfield. Third row: Ivy Cooper, Emily Mayos, Doreen Brookfield, Jean Mayos, Ken Smith, Pauline Cooper, Jean Memmot, Joyce Bristow, Mary Timms, Jean Burnett. Bottom row: John Bramall, Doug Thompson, Brian Betts, Keith Timms, Malcolm Gillot.

The Festival of Britain Parade, 1951. Reg Waterhouse with his decorated horse and wagon. Its occupants are Underbank Chapel May queen Audrey Wallis, with her attendants Hazel Bramall (left) and Margaret Robinson (right).

The Festival of Britain Parade, 1951. From left to right: the small boy is Graham Crapper, next to local schoolteacher Miss Hoole. On float: Lynn Furness, Vivienne Simons, –?–, Ruth Standing, Shirley Fellowes, Maureen Gosney. Rear: festival queen Gillian Hodgkinson.

Rag Day, 1951. Keith Turner on the wagon of his grandfather, Joseph Turner.

Coronation Day Parade, 2 June 1953. Front: Joe Turner. Walking behind is Fred Flewitt, leading his horse and wagon with crown, on Oldfield Road.

The May 1953 pageant for the Coronation at Stannington Council School. Pictured is the full cast including back row: Britannia (Lynn Hopkins); back right: St George (Gordon Revitt); centre back: Queen Elizabeth I (Sylvia Smith); centre front: courtier (Gloria Hallam).

Stannington Co-op Women's Guild on an outing to Josiah Wedgewood's factory at Barlaston, plus coach driver George Nichols (front left), and Mr Ronksley and Wilson Smith (front right). The trip was organised by Mrs Ronksley, fourth from left in the front.

The Royal British Legion's Poppy Appeal in the early 1980s, taken in the Hare and Hounds. From left to right, back row: John Maitland, Leslie Banks, Alec Taylor, -?-, Barry Hartley, George Baker, Cecil Griffiths, Ernest Goodison, Ken Wilmott, George White, Joe Atkins, ? Johnson. Front row: -?-, -?-, Nora White, Mrs Wilmott, George Walker, Joyce Johnson.

Stannington school children find a civil war cannon ball on Catty Lane in March, 1965. From left to right: Alan Frogatt, Jane Marples, Julie Chapman.

The full cast of a production of *Macbeth*, March 1952, including Eric and Margaret Chapman and Brian Stead, who were involved with the formation of the Stannington Players.

But Once A Year, performed December 1961. Stannington Players are, from left to right, back row: Renee Faulkner, Nora Maitland, Marion Smith, Frank Totty, Eric Faulkner. Front row: Valarie Retter, -?-, -?-.

Right: The Wizard of Oz production, December 1967, by Stannington Players. From left to right: Mark Lupton, Denise Robinson, Peter Davies, John Hudson, Margaret Bird and Stuart Baines.

Below: Stannington Players' production of *Mystery at Greenfingers*, 1977. From left to right, back row: Helen Roebuck, Stephen Rhodes, Barbara Kerfoot, Welwyn D'Roza. Front row: Linda Smith, Edna Richardson, Stephen Packard.

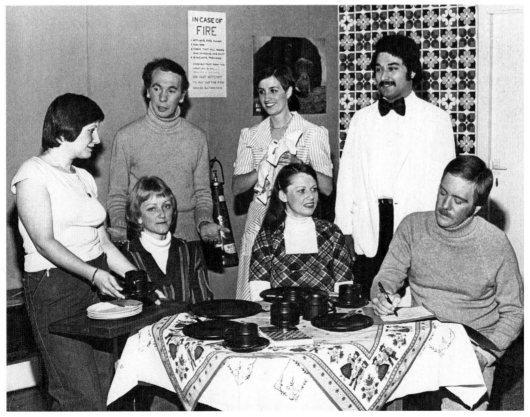

Right: Cakin' night at the Crown and Glove, Stannington on 1 November, 1989. Such competitions were held for the best disguises/costumes. The aim was not to be recognised, as forfeits must be paid out to the competitor in goods or money. This is held on 1 November only.

Below: Stannington carol singers at the home of Mrs Betty Wilson on Christmas Eve 1978. From left to right: Roger Wilson, Steve Flewitt, Vivian Crapper, Nick Farrelly, Belfield Furness, Ernest Goodison (Father Christmas), Betty Wilson, Peter Ramsey, Joe Atkins.

The local history group committee at the fortieth anniversary Christmas party, December 2002. From left to right are: Jean Broadhead, John Wilde, Doug Broadhead, Joy Allen-Sissons, Norma Reaney, Pauline Plant, Brian Holder, Sylvia Wragg, Len Johnson and Joe Atkins.

If you are interested in purchasing other books published by The History Press, or in case you have difficulty finding any of our books in your local bookshop, you can also place orders directly through our website
www.thehistorypress.co.uk